Contents

What is pulling? 4

How can you pull
    something heavy? 6

How hard do you have to pull? 10

Can you pull something
    heavier than you? 14

Can you pull down to pull
    something up? 18

Quiz 22

Glossary 23

Index 24

Answer to quiz 24

What is pulling?

Pulling is one way to move something towards you.

You can pull your toy to move it.

Pulling

Patricia Whitehouse

www.raintreepublishers.co.uk
Visit our website to find out more information about **Raintree** books.

To order:
☎ Phone 44 (0) 1865 888112
🖹 Send a fax to 44 (0) 1865 314091
🖥 Visit the Raintree Bookshop at **www.raintreepublishers.co.uk** to browse our catalogue and order online.

First published in Great Britain by Raintree, Halley Court, Jordan Hill, Oxford OX2 8EJ, part of Harcourt Education.
Raintree is a registered trademark of Harcourt Education Ltd.

Editorial: Nick Hunter and Diyan Leake
Design: Michelle Lisseter
Picture Research: Beth Chisholm
Production: Lorraine Hicks

Originated by Dot Gradations
Printed and bound in China by South China Printing Company

ISBN 1 844 21551 2 (hardback)
07 06 05 04
10 9 8 7 6 5 4 3 2

ISBN 1 844 21557 1 (paperback)
08 07 06 05 04
10 9 8 7 6 5 4 3 2 1

British Library Cataloguing in Publication Data
Whitehouse, Patricia
Pulling
531
A full catalogue record for this book is available from the British Library.

Acknowledgements
The publishers would like to thank the following for permission to reproduce photographs: Corbis/Ariel Skelley, 5; Heinemann Library/Que-Net, 4, 6, 7, 8, 9, 10, 11, 12, 13, 14, 15, 16, 17, 22, 23, 24; Heinemann Library/Robert Lifson, 18, 19, 20, 21

Cover photograph reproduced with permission of Rolf Bruderer/Corbis.

Every effort has been made to contact copyright holders of any material reproduced in this book. Any omissions will be rectified in subsequent printings if notice is given to the publishers.

Some words are shown in bold, **like this**. They are explained in the glossary on page 23.

Some things are easy to pull.

Other things are hard to pull.

How can you pull something heavy?

This toy box is full.

You need to pull it away from the wall.

Try to pull the toy box with your hands.

Is it easy to do?

Now put a **handle** on the toy box.

What will happen when you pull on the handle?

A handle makes things easier to pull.

How hard do you have to pull?

This box is full of building bricks.

You need to take it to another room.

Try to pull the box.

You have to pull hard to move the box over the **rough** carpet.

Now the box is on the **smooth** floor.

How hard will you have to pull?

You do not have to pull very hard.

The box is easier to pull on a smooth floor.

Can you pull something heavier than you?

This box of books is heavy.

How can you move it?

Tie a **handle** on to the box.

It is still too heavy to pull.

Ask a friend to help you.

Will you be able to pull the box now?

More people means more
pulling power.

You can pull the box together!

Can you pull down to pull something up?

Your friend is on top of the bridge.

Can you give her something to eat?

You can tie a rope to a basket of fruit.

How does the rope help?

Throw one end of the rope over the railing.

Now, pull down gently on the rope.

When you pull down, the basket goes up.

Your friend can have a piece of fruit.

Quiz

Will the toy be easier to pull through the **rough** grass or across the **smooth** pavement?

Look for the answer on page 24.

Glossary

handle
part used to pick up, open or hold something

rough
uneven or bumpy surface

smooth
even surface that is not bumpy or rough

Index

basket   19, 21

books   14

box   10, 11, 12,
   13, 14, 15, 16, 17

bricks   10

carpet   11

floor   12, 13

friend   16, 18, 21

fruit   19, 21

handle   8, 9, 15, 23

rope   19, 20

toy   4, 22

toy box   6, 7, 8

Answer to quiz on page 22

It is easier to pull the toy on the smooth pavement.

 CAUTION: Children should not attempt any experiment without an adult's help and permission.